James Robertson

James Robertson was born in Kent in 1958, but grew up in Bridge of Allan in Stirlingshire. He studied history at Edinburgh University, at both undergraduate and postgraduate levels. His first book of short stories, *Close*, was published in 1991 by Black & White Publishing. In 1993 he was appointed writer-in-residence at Brownsbank Cottage, the former home of the poet Hugh MacDiarmid, near Biggar in Lanarkshire. During his two-year stay there he published a second book of stories, *The Ragged Man's Complaint* (1993) and a collection of poems, *Sound-Shadow* (1995). He also edited the collection of contemporary short stories in Scots, *A Tongue in Yer Heid* (1994) and two books by the 19th-century geologist and folklorist Hugh Miller. *Scottish Ghost Stories* appeared in 1996, as did a *Dictionary of Scottish Quotations* which he co-compiled with Angela Cran. In 1999 he set up the pamphlet imprint Kettillonia, publishing poetry and short fiction by various authors. His own poetry, including *I Dream of Alfred Hitchcock* (1999), *Fae the Flouers o Evil: Baudelaire in Scots* (2001) and *Stirling Sonnets* (2001), has appeared under the Kettillonia imprint. He produced a new edition of the *Selected Poems* of Robert Fergusson in 2000 to mark the 250th anniversary of the poet's birth. He is general editor of the Scots language educational imprint Itchy Coo, for which he wrote *A Scots Parliament* (2002). His first novel, *The Fanatic*, was published by Fourth Estate in 2000. His second, *Joseph Knight*, won both the Saltire and Scottish Arts Council Book of the Year Awards for 2003–04. He lives in Angus.

Further information:
www.itchy-coo.com
www.kettillonia.co.uk

voyage of intent

voyage of intent

Sonnets and Essays
from the Scottish Parliament

James Robertson

strangefruit

**Scottish Book Trust, July 2005
Co-published with Luath Press**

Luath Press Ltd

Acknowledgements

Published by Scottish Book Trust and Luath Press to mark the first ever writer-in-residency at the Scottish Parliament in November 2004.

Scottish **Book** Trust

Luath Press Ltd

Sandeman House
Trunk's Close
55 High Street
Edinburgh EH1 1SR
0131 524 0160
www.scottishbooktrust.com

ISBN: 1-905222-26-2

© James Robertson, 2005.
Enric Miralles artwork © Scottish Parliamentary Corporate Body.
Photography © Niall Hendrie. Photography by permission of SPCB.
Designed by Emma Quinn.
Printed by twentyonecolour, Glasgow
All rights reserved.

Thanks to Carcanet for permission to reproduce Edwin Morgan's 'The Coin'
and to Polygon for permission to reproduce 'Old Edinburgh' and 'Patriot'
by Norman MacCaig. *The Poems of Norman MacCaig* is available now
ISBN 1904598269.

Scottish Book Trust gratefully acknowledges the invaluable help
of John Gibbons and Eric Kinsey from the Holyrood Project Team.

Thanks also to the Presiding Officer George Reid and Laura Davey and
Alan Rennie at the Scottish Parliament.

A *strangefruit* production from Scottish Book Trust
"Appetite grows by eating" (Rabelais)

Citizens
sitting, resting.

For my father

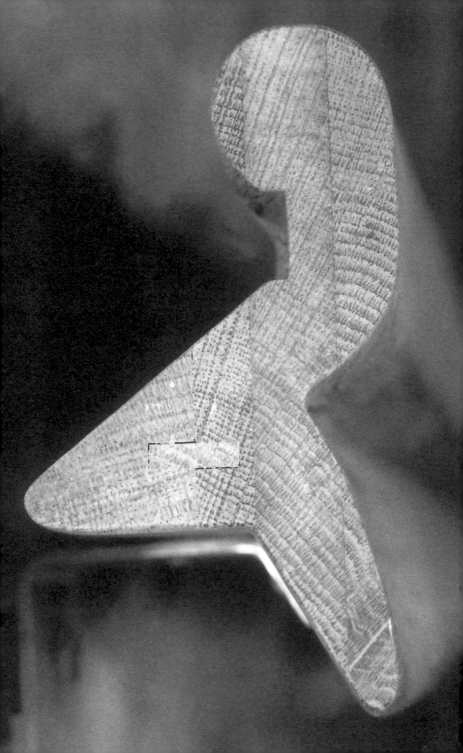

contents

voyage of intent
Sonnets and Essays from the Scottish Parliament

I had no idea, when I accepted Scottish Book Trust's invitation to be the first writer "in residence" in the Scottish Parliament, what my creative response would be to the building and the people who work in it. I agreed to write and deliver three talks – given to MSPs, their staff and the staff of the Parliament itself – on the historical relationship between Scottish politics and literature, on literary descriptions of that part of Edinburgh where the Parliament is located, and on how writers over the centuries have responded to the vexed question of Scottish identity. These talks are reproduced here and as it turns out they form a context for the other part of my remit, which was to write something arising out of my experience at Holyrood. But at the time I did not know what this piece of writing would be, nor what thoughts and feelings might inform it.

The eleven sonnets that emerged are like snapshots of the Parliament a few weeks after its official opening. There is a kind of story running through them, beginning with the architect and how the physical shape of his building grew from quite abstract ideas about land, nation and politics; then moving on to some of the specific aspects and motifs of the building itself; then observing the reactions and behaviours of the visiting public and newly installed MSPs; then, through the figures of Belhaven and Fergusson, connecting past to present and future; and finally returning to the idea of a parliament being much more than simply a building. This story developed subconsciously as the sonnets took shape. It was also by accident rather than intention that the poems ended up containing so much imagery of boats and water – perhaps a result of the "subtle implications" of Enric Miralles's inspiring architecture. But another writer would probably have taken an entirely different set of pictures.

I arrived at the Parliament sceptical about both its location and design. I left it filled with admiration for the building, and very conscious of the energy and enthusiasm that it seems to generate in those who work in it – some eleven hundred people in all, including the MSPs. It is not what one might expect a parliament to look like, and this is one of its strengths. It is impressive rather than magnificent, stylish rather than grand, humorous rather than staid, welcoming rather than imposing, celebratory rather than monumental. It invites comment and challenges preconceptions. It is a series of surprises, an assemblage of connected phrases rather than one big, bombastic statement. It honours history but projects itself into the future. It makes you think. It seems right for 21st-century Scotland.

James Robertson

The Vision of Enric Miralles *(1)*

A subtle game of views and implications
is what I play. Once, Edinburgh was this:
a mountain and some buildings, synthesis
of human and geological formations.
What we create must fit with what's on hand –
cut through the Old Town's grain and yet enhance,
be mindful of the past, and yet advance –
a Parliament that sits within the land,
a gathering where land and people meet.
The land itself will be a building-block:
to me this is of greatest consequence.
The Parliament will grow from Arthur's Seat,
a bridge between the city and the rock,
a mirror of the land it represents.

The Vision of Enric Miralles *(2)*

I think of Scotland and I think of boats.
Always these boats are present in my mind,
and by their shapes the building is defined:
a Parliament on land and yet it floats;
a set of shelters under upturned keels,
an anchorage, a point of embarkation,
a source of new light for an old dark nation,
a place of thoughts, ambitions and ideals.
But all they want to know – how much? and when?
as if the future will not pay or wait.
I tell them it will cost what it will cost,
be finished when it's finished, not till then.
Why do they only call *too dear, so late*
that which for three whole centuries was lost?

That Shape

A hairdryer, wind turbine, mason's bolster,
a Clydeside crane, inquisitive grey seal,
a Highland woman bent beneath her creel,
an anvil, mallet, drill, hand-gun in holster,
tin-opener, boy bugler, shaft of coal-pit,
boat's keel and rudder, shadow of giraffe,
iron head of niblick, divot left by sclaff,
ice-skating minister, his empty pulpit,
Munro-bagger, head lowered into gale,
discarded welly lying on its side,
gathering cyclone, cloud of rising geese,
the lofted tail-flukes of a diving whale,
a photo of the soul of Mr Hyde,
an abstract map of Scotland by Matisse.

The MSPs' Wing

Outside, a fleet of boats against the sky,
Fifies maybe, jostling for fish and space,
or, bamboo-rigged, cutters or junks that race
across a hard grey-granite sea, six storeys high.
This bold flotilla crowds the eastward view,
all cabins, crow-stepped fo'c'sles, sterns and prows,
vessels that might be scaffies, brigs or dhows –
but not a passenger in sight, and where's the crew?
Inside, like monks and nuns in contemplation
on some great ocean-going kirk,
the MSPs dream in their port-holed pods,
repair the cracks of recent navigation,
or chart new routes for health or schools or work –
humble as tars, or vain as little gods.

Signage

oh there wis a right stushie ower the signs
first they wrote aw that bloody gaelic oot
naebody seems tae ken whit that's aboot
i mean the warld speaks english noo aye mine's
a whisky pal here's tae us slainte cheers
then some folk wantit slang aw ower the shop
weel nane o that or whaur the hell d'ye stop
next ye'd hae chimps up in the chandeliers
whit's that ye say nae chandeliers aw wait
a minute noo wi aw thae millions spent
nae chandeliers jist shows ye eh nae cless
and ken doon on the pavement at the gate
they've peyed some clown tae write in the cement
some shite aboot angels and tungs and bress

The People

The public foyer fills with people, here
to see what's been created in their name.
They come in hundreds every day, to claim
possession of the place. The atmosphere
buzzes with energy, people are seeing
their aspirations finally made real,
expressed in glass and granite, oak and steel;
their *settled will* brought into concrete being.
Too naïve a view? Cynics may deride,
but something in these faces fills the heart,
potent and moving yet inexplicit.
Relief perhaps, surprise, a little pride,
a sense of closure, and of a new start?
This is ours, they are saying, *this is it.*

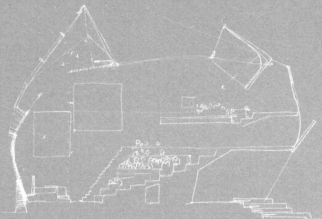

The Debating Chamber

Under the massive beams and banks of lights
the oak and sycamore's pale, sweeping grace
gives a grove-like quality to the place
as, outside, the afternoon fills with night's
dark ink. In the gallery a school group
quietly leaves. Others (young and old) sit
listening to the debate below. As it
begins to wind up, the MSPs troop
in, take their seats. Something ancient and weird
is in this tribal play, as if instinct
and ritual have combined, free will and rote;
as if we all have somehow reappeared
after long sleep, to find ourselves still linked
to the thought, to the process, to the vote.

A Manifesto for MSPs

Dinna be glaikit, dinna be ower smert,
dinna craw croose, dinna be unco blate,
dinna breenge in, dinna be ayewis late,
dinna steek yer lugs, dinna steek yer hert.
Dinna be sleekit, dinna be a sook,
dinna creesh nae loof for future favour,
dinna swick nor swither, hash nor haiver,
dinna be soor o face, and dinna jouk.
Open yer airms and minds tae folk in need,
hain frae fylin and skaith the land and sea,
tak tent o justice and the commonweal,
ding doon hypocrisy, wanthrift and greed,
heeze up the banner o humanity,
seek oot the truth and tae the truth be leal.

In Our Name

None can destroy Scotland, save Scotland's self;
hold your hands from the pen, you are secure.
Belhaven, rejecting the Union's lure,
could not dissuade those hands from grasping pelf,
preferment, empire, trade and all the rest.
No doubt some made an honest computation,
thought it the right and best thing for the nation:
the trick is how you measure right and best.
Now, Holyrood, if in these brave new times
it seems politic to avert your gaze
when powers reserved to Westminster include
bombing Iraq and other, lesser crimes,
resist all bowing, scraping, grasping ways:
dissent like Belhaven, do not collude.

Fergusson's Statue

Ye're stridin doon the Canongate, brent new
and lookin like ye've never been awa,
were never found curled deid upon the straw
in Bedlam's cells; ye're twenty-fower and fou –
no claret-fou, but o yersel and life,
rat-rhymes and habbies rattlin through yer heid,
a book in haun, and hunners mair tae read –
the warld is yours, at least as faur as Fife.
Ye'd ken and yet ye widna ken yer toun:
some gains ye'd praise, some losses ye'd lament –
sae muckle change, sae muckle aye the same.
Auld Reikie's still as braw beneath the moon,
and noo we even hae oor Parliament,
come hame like you, Rob Fergusson, come hame.

The Voyage

And if or when the people's surge subsides
to tourist trickles from this present spate,
do not relax or quietly desiccate,
do not raise dykes against their future tides:
push out your boats onto the rising seas
of all their desolations, hopes, needs, dreams,
flooding the city streets and housing schemes,
the hospitals, schools, farms and factories.
For in the end a Parliament is not
a building, but a voyage of intent,
a journey to whatever we might be.
This is our new departure, this is what
we opted for, solid and permanent,
yet tenuous with possibility.

notes

The Vision of Enric Miralles (1) and (2)

These sonnets are based on some of the Catalan architect's statements contained in the original submissions to the architectural competition and in later documents, and on comments he made at various stages of the project. I am grateful to Dr John Gibbons, Architectural Adviser to the Scottish Parliament, for his detailed and enthusiastic explanation of some of the thinking behind the design.

Signage

Some consideration was given to the possibility of the Parliament's signs being tri-lingual, in English, Gaelic and Scots, but despite protests from the Scots Language lobby only English and Gaelic were used. This sonnet is an ironic take on this issue. The reference to "angels and tungs and bress" refers to the inscription at the Queensberry House entrance taken from W.L. Lorimer's New Testament in Scots, 1 Corinthians chapter 13: "Gin I speak wi the tungs o men an angels, but hae nae luve i my hairt, I am no nane better nor dunnerin bress or a rínging cymbal."

The People

The "settled will of the Scottish people" was a phrase used by the late John Smith to describe their commitment to some form of devolution. In the first nine weeks of the Parliament being open to the public, it received 100,000 visitors.

In Our Name

The opening lines are a direct quotation from an impassioned speech against the Union made by John Hamilton, Lord Belhaven (1656–1708), in the Scottish Parliament on 2nd November 1706. His words were recorded by Daniel Defoe in his History of the Union.

Fergusson's Statue

Robert Fergusson (1750–1774) was a poet who captured the life of Edinburgh in the 1770s in a series of brilliant poems written in Scots, before dying in miserable circumstances in the city madhouse or Bedlam. The sonnet mentions "habbies", Standard Habbie being the six-line stanza form much used by Allan Ramsay, Fergusson and Robert Burns. There is also a reference to the lines in Fergusson's poem celebrating his native city, Auld Reikie: "Auld Reikie! wale o' ilka toun / That Scotland kens beneath the moon". A bronze statue of Fergusson by David Annand was unveiled on 17th October 2004, the anniversary of his death, on the pavement outside the Canongate kirkyard, where he is buried.

The Voyage

This sonnet draws on a remark made by Enric Miralles in an explanatory document on the design of the Parliament: "The new parliament building will be a significant moment in the history of the Scottish Nation... But a Parliament is not a building... it is one of the formal aspects of a political organisation..."

masterclasses

1 A Parcel of Rogues

Robert Burns (1759–96) famously denounced the Scots Parliamentarians who voted for the Treaty of Union with England in 1707, as a "parcel of rogues". But politicians have been castigated and mocked by writers for centuries – in fact, you could say that such abuse comes with the job. The relationship between Scottish politics and literature has not always been easy, but it has positive as well as negative aspects.

"There's ane end of ane auld sang," the Chancellor, the Earl of Seafield, disparagingly said as he signed the Treaty. His anti-Union opponent, Andrew Fletcher of Saltoun, had three years earlier written that "if a man were permitted to make all the ballads, he need not care who should make the laws of a nation" – an opinion now inscribed on the wall of the new Parliament. With Scotland lacking its own legislature, the nation's ballad-makers, poets and, later, novelists did in a way come to be, along with the Kirk and the Law, a substitute political voice. Maybe this is one reason why we still attach such value to the words of Robert Burns, and why, in the 19th century in particular, the poems and novels of Sir Walter Scott became the window through which the outside world saw Scotland.

"We're bought and sold for English gold", was Burns's bitter denunciation of the Union, and his song 'A Parcel of Rogues in a Nation' deplores the idea of Scotland becoming a mere province of its southern neighbour. What really upset Burns was that Scotland's hard fought for, centuries-old independence was signed away by a small group of men who were entrusted with determining national policy and laws but who seemed to put their own interests above those of the country:

> What force or guile could not subdue
> Thro' many warlike ages
> Is wrought now by a coward few
> For hireling traitors' wages.

Although this view – that bribes were the principal reason for Scots MPs agreeing to the Union – oversimplifies things, it was shared by the bulk of the population. No other single political moment in Scottish history has stirred such emotions among our poets and songwriters, both at the time and long after. Burns was writing eighty-five years after the event. In 1707 the Gaelic poet Iain Lom (John Macdonald, c.1620–c.1707) scathingly addressed Highland chiefs like Lord Duplin whose "heart wildly beat / when you heard gold was coming":

shluig thu 'n aileag den gheanach,
dh'at do sgamhan is bhòc e,
dh'fhosgail teannsgal do ghoile
's lasaich greallag do thòna.

Oran an Aghaidh an Aonaidh

(you stifled greed's breath
till your lungs swelled and hiccuped,
till you could not contain it
and set light to your arsehole.)

A Song Against the Union

Meanwhile, an anonymous 'Litanie Anent the Union' laid into almost every feature of Scottish affairs and government:

From heavie taxes laid on salt,
On blinkèd ale, on beer or malt,   [blinkèd: sour]
And herrying us without a fault...

From trading with an emptie purse
And meriting the old wife's curse,
And from all changes to the worse...

From bartering the ancient nation
For a new trade communication,
From English acts of navigation,
Deliver us, Lord.

Decades later, the Church of Scotland minister turned playwright John Home (1722–1808) suggested, tongue in cheek, a simpler reason for Scotland's decline:

> Firm and erect the Caledonian stood;
> Old was his mutton, and his claret good.
> "Let him drink port!" an English statesman cried;
> He drank the poison, and his spirit died.

> *Epigram on Enforcement of High Duty on French Wines*

Blaming the English for Scottish woes is a habit with a long pedigree, but there was another, at least as old, of criticising Scottish kings, courtiers and Parliamentarians for failing to perform their duties properly. In pre-Union Scotland the most famous example of a piece of literature confronting political mismanagement and corruption was the play *Ane Satyre of the Thrie Estaitis*, written by Sir David Lyndsay (c.1486–1555), himself a courtier during the reign of James V and the minority of Mary. Lyndsay was building on the legacy of earlier great poets or makars, such as Robert Henryson (c.1420–c.1490), William Dunbar (c.1460–c.1520) and Gavin Douglas (c.1474–1522), who had variously used allegories, satires, and poems of petition and of complaint, to make political points. "Gude rewle is banist ouer the Bordour" Dunbar had lamented in one of his poems, and Lyndsay's play takes up the theme. It concerns King Humanitie, who is diverted from ruling his people well by such characters as Wantonness, Flatterie and Dame Sensualitie. Eventually Divyne Correctioun arrives to restore order and suggests the summoning of the three Estates of the realm – the clergy, nobility and burgesses – to a Parliament. But the Parliament itself is corrupt and confused, the Estates entering the stage backwards to signify their poor condition. Meanwhile the ordinary people and the wellbeing of the whole country are represented by John the Commonweill. Through humour as well as moralising Lyndsay analyses the right balance of power necessary to maintain justice, liberty and prosperity in a country such as Scotland.

The ceremony and processions in Lyndsay's play had their basis in reality. The tradition of the Riding of the Parliament, revived in our own time, goes back many centuries. It was an opportunity for people to view their representatives on their way to make laws that would affect the whole nation, but the crowd was not always deferential. There was a sense, which has returned with the modern Parliament, that if the people and their representatives were within physical reach of each other, it both brought the idea of government closer to ordinary lives and concentrated the minds of the politicians. Sir Walter Scott (1771–1832), in his novel *The Heart of Midlothian*, set in 1736, captures this idea through his character Mrs Howden, in words also now set in stone at Holyrood:

> "I dinna ken muckle about the law," answered Mrs Howden;
> "but I ken, when we had a king, and a chancellor, and parliament-men o' our ain, we could aye peeble them wi' stanes if they werena gude bairns – But naebody's nails can reach the length o' Lunnon."

Politicians in the 18th and early 19th centuries were used to getting pebbles and a good deal worse flung at them by the populace. In his novel *The Provost*, John Galt (1779–1839) has Mr Pawkie, provost of the burgh of Gudetown, describe what happens when he reads the Riot Act from a window to an angry crowd gathered below:

> ...they listened in silence. But this was a concerted stratagem; for the moment that I had ended, a dead cat came whizzing through the air like a comet, and gave me such a clash in the face that I was knocked down to the floor, in the middle of the very council-chamber.

More recently, Westminster politicians were often an easy target for our writers, especially if, like Hugh MacDiarmid (1892–1978), the writer was coming at them from both a nationalist and a communist standpoint.

In the General Election of 1964, MacDiarmid stood as a Communist Party candidate in the Kinross and West Perthshire constituency of the Conservative Prime Minister, Sir Alec Douglas-Home. He denounced Sir Alec as "a zombie, personifying the obsolescent traditions of an aristocratic and big landlord order, of which Thomas Carlyle said that no country had been oppressed by a worse gang of hyenas than Scotland." The campaign, MacDiarmid said, was a personal issue: "After all, I have a personality, and Home doesn't." There was much more of this red-blooded invective, but in spite or because of his campaign tactics MacDiarmid came bottom of the poll with 127 votes. It is said that he asked for a recount, on the grounds that "it's hard to believe there are 127 good socialists in Kinross and West Perthshire"!

Some Scottish writers, such as John Buchan (1875–1940) and Robert Bontine Cunninghame Graham (1852–1936), did actually serve as MPs at Westminster. Although a Unionist, Buchan as early as 1932 showed himself to be open-minded about Home Rule. "If it could be proved that a separate Scottish Parliament were desirable," he said, "Scotsmen should support it. I would go further. Even if it were not proved desirable, if it could be proved to be desired by any substantial majority of the Scottish people, then Scotland should be allowed to make the experiment." In Buchan's thrillers, as well as in his more profound historical novels, politics is seldom far away. "You think that a wall as solid as the earth separates civilisation from barbarism," a character says in *The Power-House*. "I tell you the division is a thread, a sheet of glass." Always aware of the importance of tradition as well as the fragility of progress, Buchan believed that "we can only pay our debt to the past by putting the future in debt to ourselves."

George Bernard Shaw remarked that Cunninghame Graham led such an incredible life that he sometimes doubted if he was real. Born into an aristocratic Stirlingshire family, he was a lifelong adventurer, travelling in North Africa and cattle-ranching in South America, as well as writing

short stories and non-fiction. At one time a Liberal MP, he was also a friend of Keir Hardie and became first president of the Scottish Labour Party on its formation; and, being a committed Home Ruler, years later he was a founder and first president of the Scottish National Party. The real enemies of Scottish nationalism, he said, were not the English, "for they were ever a great and generous folk", but those among us "born without imagination". He also said, "The strife of parties means nothing but the rotation of rascals in office", but he did believe in the power of politics to change things for the better.

So, too, did many Scottish writers in the period between the devolution referendum of 1979 and the re-establishment of the Scottish Parliament in 1999. Those two decades saw the deaths of many of the great figures of 20th-century Scottish literature: MacDiarmid had died in 1978, and Norman MacCaig, Sorley MacLean, Iain Crichton Smith and Naomi Mitchison ("Nobody," Mitchison said, "can be a power in their age unless they are part of its voice"), all of whom were in favour of a Scottish Parliament, passed on before it was achieved. But there was also a resurgence of interest in the Scottish literature of the past, a renewed commitment to writing in Gaelic and Scots, and a wave of new writers, most of whom wanted some change in Scotland's political status. Much of the cultural regeneration of Scotland that preceded the referendum vote of 1997 – which made it quite clear that, in John Buchan's words, a substantial majority of the Scottish people desired their own Parliament – was instigated by writers. And there lies the positive side of the relationship between politics and literature. Writers will, with rare exceptions, never be politicians; but in their work they express political desires and dissatisfactions; they depict the real state of a country as well as imagining past and future states; they criticise and they applaud; they raise hopes and aspirations; and they are often called upon by the media to comment on some aspect or other of the nation's life. In all these ways, they are as essential to the "common-weill" of Scotland as decent, industrious and visionary politicians.

None of this takes account of those Scottish writers whose works on economics, social policy and philosophy have had a direct and lasting effect on politicians throughout the world. These might include, for example, Adam Smith, author of *The Wealth of Nations*, David Hume (1711–76) and Patrick Geddes (1854–1932). But the last word here must go to Scotland's Makar, Edwin Morgan (1920–), whose poem 'Open the Doors!', written to mark the opening of the new Parliament building, is a manifesto for writers, politicians and all Scotland's citizens:

> What do the people want of the place?
> They want it to be filled with thinking people
> as open and adventurous as its architecture.
> A nest of fearties is what they do not want.
> A symposium of procrastinators is what they do not want.
> A phalanx of forelock-tuggers is what they do not want.
> And perhaps above all the droopy mantra of "it wizny me"
>   is what they do not want.
> Dear friends, dear lawgivers, dear parliamentarians,
> you are picking up a thread of pride and self-esteem
> that has been almost but not quite, oh no not quite,
> not ever broken or forgotten...
> We give you our consent to govern, don't pocket it and ride away.
> We give you our deepest dearest wish to govern well,
> don't say we have no mandate to be so bold.
> We give you this great building,
> don't let your work and hope be other than great
> when you enter and begin.
> So now begin. Open the doors and begin.

2 The Gable-Ends o' Time

For centuries Edinburgh's Old Town has been the heart of Scotland's cultural, political, legal, religious and civic life. Geology (the Royal Mile lies on a ridge of sedimentary rock protected from the west-east flow of glaciers during the Ice Age by the harder volcanic plinth on which the Castle sits) and humanity (the site has been continuously inhabited by people for perhaps seven thousand years) have combined to create a place that is like no other. While it is true that the building of the New Town gave Edinburgh a physical appearance that seemed to reflect its divided nature, all the contradictions and confusions, bright spaces and dark corners of that nature already existed in the Old Town, where, according to Oliver Goldsmith (1730–74) in the 1750s, "you might see a well-dressed duchess issuing from a dirty close", and where in the 1780s Deacon William Brodie would dine with respectable citizens by day and go house-breaking with his gang by night.

What the growth of Edinburgh away from its original centre did was to accentuate the differences; and writers, consciously or not, have seized on those differences in their work. Without the contrast between the Old Town and suburbs like Morningside and Newington we would not have had Muriel Spark's Miss Jean Brodie; without the schemes, like Pilton and Muirhouse, that grew beyond the suburbs, we would not have had Irvine Welsh's Renton and Begbie. But it is with the Old Town itself, and especially the High Street and Canongate that form the Royal Mile, that we are presently concerned.

Today, as ever, history stretches the length of the "guttit haddie" from the Castle to Holyrood, but there is a new chapter at its foot. The site of the modern Parliament was, and will perhaps continue to be, the subject of much debate, but there is undoubtedly a certain poetry about its location. It has taken its place in a crammed, bustling cityscape that endlessly breathes tradition while also constantly re-inventing itself. No other patch of Scotland has inspired so many words from so many writers, although much of what they have written is far from complimentary.

As early as the late 15th century William Dunbar was imploring Edinburgh's merchants to clean up their "nobill toun":

> May nane pas throw your principall gaittis [gaittis: streets]
> For stink of haddockis and of scattis,
> For cryis of carlingis and debaittis, [carlingis: old fishwives]
> For feusum flyttingis of defame: [feusum flyttingis: foul quarrelling]
> Think ye not schame,
> Befoir strangeris of all estaittis
> That sic dishonour hurt your name?
>
> *To the Merchantis of Edinburgh*

And this is a theme that has persisted ever since. In the 1720s the English traveller Edmund Burt (d.1755) found the squalor of "Auld Reikie" almost unbearable. The cook at the inn he stayed in was "too filthy an Object to be described, only another English Gentleman whispered me, and said, he believed, if the Fellow was to be thrown against the Wall, he would stick to it." Fifty years later, Robert Fergusson (1750–74) gleefully celebrated the things that Burt and other visitors found so off-putting, including the emptying of chamber-pots, the infamous "flooers o Edinburgh", into the street:

> On stair wi tub, or pat in hand,
> The barefoot housemaids loo to stand,
> That antrin fock may ken how snell
> Auld Reikie will at morning smell:
> Then, with an inundation big as
> The burn that 'neath the Nore Loch brig is,
> They kindly shower Edina's roses,
> To quicken and regale our noses.
>
> *Auld Reikie*

Thomas Carlyle (1795–1881), in a letter to his brother in 1821, described Edinburgh as "this accursed, stinking, reeky mass of stones and lime and dung". And Robert Louis Stevenson (1850–94), in his *Edinburgh: Picturesque Notes* of 1878–9, wrote of the Old Town as a "black labyrinth" which, though "well washed with rain all the year round", had "a grim and sooty aspect among its younger suburbs". "You go under dark arches, and down dark stairs and alleys. The way is so narrow that you can lay a hand on either wall; so steep that, in greasy winter weather, the pavement is almost as treacherous as ice."

This physical sense of descending into gloom, and simultaneously into history, is perhaps what makes the old quarter of Edinburgh such a compelling backdrop for modern crime fiction. The father-figure of detectives, Sherlock Holmes, was the invention of an Edinburgh writer, Sir Arthur Conan Doyle (1859–1930), but Holmes was of course based in London. On the other hand, Ian Rankin's Inspector Rebus, Alanna Knight's Victorian Inspector Faro, Quentin Jardine's Bob Skinner, and Paul Johnston's 21st-century cop Quintillian Dalrymple have all investigated crimes in or around the Royal Mile. "You get the great perpendiculars of the Old Town that hint at the heights of human achievement, at the same time as the rapid descent to the inferno below", Johnston has commented. Knight is interested in "the difference in morality between 'respectable' Edinburgh and its darker, seedier elements". "As a city," Jardine writes in *Skinner's Rules*, "Edinburgh is a two-faced bitch".

All these sentiments echo Stevenson rather than Conan Doyle. Stevenson grew up in the relatively sedate New Town but was drawn as a student to the howffs and dens of the Old Town. His classic novel of the divided self, *The Strange Case of Dr Jekyll and Mr Hyde*, may be set in London, but there is no mistaking its origins in the career of Deacon Brodie and the topography of Auld Reikie. From earliest memory, Stevenson's affection for his native city was tempered by disgust: "I seem to have been born with a sentiment of something moving in things, of an infinite attraction and horror coupled." Yet the reverse of that dark repulsion was the surprise and hope that Edinburgh is to this day still capable of delivering: "You peep under an arch, you descend stairs that look as if they would land you in a cellar, you turn to the back-window of a grimy tenement in a lane: – and behold! you are face-to-face with distant and bright prospects. You turn a corner, and there is the sun going down into the Highland hills. You look down an alley, and see ships tacking for the Baltic."

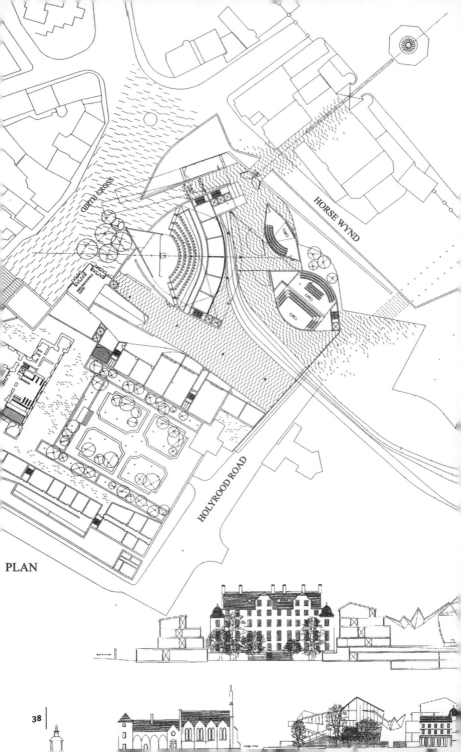

PLAN

CUTH CROSS

HORSE WYND

HOLYROOD ROAD

Some of the most memorable scenes in Scottish literature are set in and around the High Street and Canongate. Sir Walter Scott's sprawling novel *The Heart of Midlothian* begins there, and in the vivid opening chapters the city itself becomes almost a living participant in the Porteous Riots of 1736. Scott portrayed old Edinburgh over and over again, in his epic poem *Marmion* and novels like *The Antiquary* and *Guy Mannering*, the latter set in the 1780s when "the great bulk of the better classes, and particularly those connected with the law, still lived in flats or dungeons of the Old Town". Mr Pleydell, the lawyer whom Colonel Mannering first encounters in a tavern on a Saturday night playing "the ancient and now forgotten pastime of High Jinks", is clearly influenced by his surroundings when he remarks, "In civilised society, law is the chimney through which all that smoke discharges itself that used to circulate through the whole house, and put every one's eyes out – no wonder, therefore, that the vent itself should sometimes get a little sooty." His lively mind is entirely at home amid the twists and turns of the Old Town:

> And away walked Mr Pleydell with great activity, diving through closes and ascending covered stairs, in order to attain the High Street by an access, which, compared to the common route, was what the Straits of Magellan are to the more open, but circuitous passage round Cape Horn.

Look at a map of South America and the aptness of Scott's analogy is immediately seen.

Scott's contemporary James Hogg (1770–1835) captured the atmosphere in a different way, in *The Private Memoirs and Confessions of a Justified Sinner*, with his disturbing description of George Colwan being stalked by his malevolent half-brother Robert "in the gallery of the Parliament House, in the boxes of the play-house, in the church, in the assembly, in the streets, suburbs, and the fields"; all of which leads to a confrontation between them in the mist on the summit of Arthur's Seat.

Hogg's novel is full of nightmarish mystery, the product, at least in part, of its Edinburgh location. There is a confluence of reality and fantasy in the Old Town, an inter-lacing of the ancient with the modern, that is a constant spur to the imagination. The precision of law is enveloped by the fog of legend through which poke the insistent reminders of history: "This rortie wretched city / Built on history / Built of history", as Sydney Goodsir Smith (1915–75) put it. This may be the domain of the Court of Session, the City Chambers, Dynamic Earth and now the concrete, glass and granite curves and angles of the Parliament, but it is also filled with echoes and glimpses of Brodie, Burke and Hare, Major Weir, Jenny Geddes, Rizzio, John Knox, James Boswell and Edinburgh's own laureate Robert Fergusson.

Fergusson was the direct heir of a revival in Scots verse begun by the wigmaker turned bookseller Allan Ramsay (1684–1758). Ramsay published collections of medieval Scots poetry, including work by William Dunbar (mentioned earlier), and generated a widespread interest in Scotland's literary heritage. He wrote verse of his own, of varying quality, and established the first circulating library in Britain, in 1736, in the Luckenbooths in the shadow of St Giles. He also, briefly, opened a theatre in Carruber's Close, but the magistrates closed it down. Ramsay might have been a one-off, but fourteen years after his death the young clerk Fergusson burst into Scots verse in *The Weekly Magazine*, prompting one reader to ask "Is Allan risen frae the deid?"

Through some sixteen poems composed in Scots between 1772 and 1773, Fergusson preserved the street life of Enlightenment Edinburgh for ever, in all its noisy, smelly, riotous variety. He is the best tour guide available if you want to sample New Year and Halloween revelries, horse-racing on Leith sands, election bevvying and brawls, the heat and din of Luckie Middlemist's oyster tavern in the Cowgate, and drunken escapes from the Lochaber axes of the town's police force, at that time mainly composed of retired Highland soldiers:

> And thou, great god of *Aqua Vitae*!
> Wha sways the empire of this city,
> When fou we're sometimes capernoity,   [capernoity: irritable]
> Be thou prepar'd,
> To hedge us frae that black banditti,
> The City Guard.

But Fergusson's exuberant verses disguised a tendency towards depression – which again perhaps reflects something of the Old Town's contradictory nature – and he died in poverty in the city Bedlam at the age of twenty-four. He, more than any other writer, influenced Robert Burns, who turned to writing in Scots on discovering Fergusson's poetry; and it was Burns who paid for a stone to be erected in the Canongate kirkyard to mark the grave of the man he called "my elder brother in misfortune, / By far my elder brother in the Muse". Over the centuries, Fergusson has continued to attract and inspire other writers, notably Stevenson ("I believe Fergusson lives in me", he claimed), Robert Garioch (1909–81) and Sydney Goodsir Smith. Finally, and fittingly within days of the opening of the new Parliament, he has reappeared on his old streets, in the form of a splendid statue by David Annand. He is hurrying down the Canongate towards Holyrood, and it is tempting to imagine that he is composing some mischievous satire on those he will find there.

What sustains the tension between tradition and innovation, between dream and reality, that seems such a part of the Old Town's character? Is it the presence of a half-wild mountain so close to the city centre? Is it the area's ability to absorb the Festival, the Fringe, ghost tours, street artists, and tens of thousands of visitors while still having an indigenous population going about its daily life? Perhaps it is simply that so much history has occurred in this ancient core of Edinburgh that nothing any more surprises it, while it continues to surprise us, its temporary residents and custodians. Norman MacCaig (1910–96) captured this in several of his poems. In 'Edinburgh Spring' he writes of the Old Town tenements at night making a "Middle Ages in the sky", a place where "Time coughs his lungs out behind a battered door":

> There craggy windows blink, mad buildings toss,
> Dishevelled roofs, and dangerous shadows lean
> Heavy with centuries, against the walls...

Or, in 'Old Edinburgh', he contrasts the triumphal progress of one image of the past with the grim crawl of another:

Down the Canongate
down the Cowgate
go vermilion dreams
snake's tongues of bannerets
trumpets with words from their mouths
saying *Praise me, praise me*.

Up the Cowgate
up the Canongate
lice on the march
tar on the amputated stump
Hell speaking with the tongue of Heaven
a woman tied to the tail of a cart.

And history leans by a dark entry
with words from his mouth
that say *Pity me, pity me*
but never forgive.

Now the core has sprouted a new Parliament, a bigger, brasher building than the old one up the hill where lawyers still perambulate beneath the hammerbeam oak roof. It has a burgeoning literary quarter too, with the Scottish Poetry Library, Scottish Book Trust and Scottish Storytelling Centre all within a short walk of Holyrood. The possibilities of Auld Reikie are endless, just as the possibilities of the Parliament are, or should be, endless. Think of the astonishing image created by Lewis Spence (1874–1955) in his poem 'The Prows o' Reekie', in which he pictures "this braw hie-heapit toun" sailing off like an enchanted ship, and anchoring at Venice, Naples or Athens:

The cruikit spell o' her backbane,
Yon shadow-mile o' spire and vane,
Wad ding them a', wad ding them a'!...

A hoose is but a puppet-box
To keep life's images frae knocks,
But mannikins scrieve oot their sauls

Upon its craw-steps and its walls:

Whaur hae they writ them mair sublime

Than on yon gable-ends o' time?

Or think of the lofty, ambitious "passionate imagining" of Hugh MacDiarmid's 1921 poem 'Edinburgh':

...Edinburgh is a mad god's dream,

Fitful and dark,

Unseizable in Leith

And wildered by the Forth,

But irresistibly at last

Cleaving to sombre heights

Of passionate imagining

Till stonily,

From soaring battlements,

Earth eyes Eternity.

Or, again, think of the challenge in Kathleen Jamie's poem of 1999 'On the Design for the New Scottish Parliament Building by Architect Enric Miralles' – a title longer than the poem itself, which simply says:

An upturned boat

– a watershed.

3 Scotland's an Attitude of Mind

What is the political and cultural identity that the new Scottish Parliament represents? Over the centuries, poets, playwrights and novelists have tried to define that identity, which would seem to be obvious but always remains elusive. Liz Lochhead's play *Mary Queen of Scots Got Her Head Chopped Off* opens with the chorus, 'La Corbie', offering a set of possible definitions:

> Country: Scotland. Whit like is it?
> It's a peatbog, it's a daurk forest,
> It's a cauldron o' lye, a saltpan or a coal mine.
> If you're gey lucky it's a bricht bere meadow or a park o' kye.
> Or mibbe... it's a field o' stanes.
> It's a tenement or a merchant's ha'.
> It's a hure hoose or a humble cot.
> Princes Street or Paddy's Merkit.
> It's a fistfu' o' fish or a pickle o' oatmeal.
> It's a queen's banquet o' roast meats and junkets.
> It depends. It depends... Ah dinna ken whit like *your* Scotland is.

It's a problem that has, naturally enough, exercised the minds of sovereigns, soldiers, diplomats, politicians, teachers, priests, property-owners, revolutionaries and football fans at least as much as writers. Over what and whom do I rule? What am I fighting/dying/killing for? What or whom do I represent? What am I trying to improve? What sense of what place am I passing on to the next generation? Does it matter at all in the larger scale and scheme of things? What is my stake in it? What is it I want to tear down, and what maintain? What am I cheering or weeping for? What is this thing called Scotland?

At one level, of course, these questions are irrelevant, as Norman MacCaig reminds us laconically in his poem 'Patriot':

My only country
is six feet high
and whether I love it or not
I'll die
for its independence.

MacCaig's great friend Hugh MacDiarmid thought otherwise, and dealt all his life in ideas of what constituted Scotland. His use of a dense form of Scots in his poetry, his kilt-wearing, whisky-drinking image, his self-acknowledged Anglophobia, his bristling, thistle-like pronouncements on every subject made him easy to caricature as a certain kind of Scotsman – "a symbol of all that's perfectly hideous about Scotland", Irvine Welsh has said of him – but in fact MacDiarmid always strove to open up the multiform possibilities of his country:

It requires great love of it deeply to read
The configuration of a land,
Gradually grow conscious of fine shadings,
Of great meanings in slight symbols...
Be like Spring, like a hand in a window
Moving New and Old things carefully to and fro,
Moving a fraction of flower here,
Placing an inch of air there,
And without breaking anything.

So I have gathered unto myself
All the loose ends of Scotland,
And by naming them and accepting them,
Loving them and identifying myself with them,
Attempt to express the whole.

Scotland

Language is an obvious means of both national and self-identification, and certainly it is not possible to engage with Scottish literature without, at some level, engaging with issues of language. Writers who write in Gaelic or Scots do so not just because these languages are theirs, but also because to use them is to make a political or cultural statement. So, Sorley MacLean (1911–96), in his great sequence of love poems *Dàin do Eimhir*, declares to his loved one how he would proclaim her "queen of Scotland" in spite of the independent socialist republic he desires:

> nan robh againn Alba shaor,
> Alba co-shinte ri ar gaol,
> Alba gheal bheadarrach fhaoil,
> Alba àlain shona laoch;
> gun bhùirdeasachd bhig chrìon bhaoith,
> gun sgreamhalachd luchd na maoin',
> 's gun chealgaireachd oillteil chlaoin,
> Alba aigeannach nan saor,
> Alba 'r fala, Alba 'r gaoil...
>
> (if we had Scotland free,
> Scotland equal to our love,
> a white spirited generous Scotland,
> a beautiful happy heroic Scotland,
> without petty paltry foolish bourgeoisie,
> without the loathsomeness of capitalists,
> without hateful crass graft;
> the mettlesome Scotland of the free,
> the Scotland of our blood, the Scotland of our love...)

Similarly, William Soutar (1898–1943), the Perth-born poet who spent the last thirteen years of his life a bed-bound invalid, wrote of an emotional connection between individual and country:

It isna but in wintry days
That wintry death is here:
It isna but on stany braes
That Scotland bides bare.

There is a cauld place in her breist
That simmer canna thaw;
A hameless place that is a waste
Whaur nae wild-fleurs blaw.

Wha has a thocht for Scotland's sake
Kens, what his bluid can tell,
That in his breist a stane maun brek
Or his hert be hale.

Heritage

MacLean's romantic, bold, passionate vision in Gaelic, and Soutar's austere one in Scots, are worlds away from that ironically delineated by Tom Buchan (1931–95) in his 'Scotland the wee':

Scotland the wee, crèche of the soul,
of thee I sing

land of the millionaire draper, whisky vomit
and the Hillman Imp

staked out with church halls, gaelic sangs
and the pan loaf

And yet all three of these visions are honest and accurate and, crucially, about the same place.

There is a telling passage in Alasdair Gray's novel *Lanark*, published in 1981, a work many regard as the book that heralded the present revival in Scottish letters. The story in *Lanark* takes place in two locations, Glasgow and the futuristic, nightmarish city of Unthank. Two characters are admiring the Glasgow skyline and have the following conversation:

"Glasgow is a magnificent city," said McAlpin. "Why do we hardly ever notice that?" "Because nobody imagines living here," said Thaw. McAlpin lit a cigarette and said, "If you want to explain that I'll certainly listen."

"Then think of Florence, Paris, London, New York. Nobody visiting them for the first time is a stranger because he's already visited them in paintings, novels, history books and films. But if a city hasn't been used by an artist not even the inhabitants live there imaginatively. What is Glasgow to most of us? A house, the place we work, a football park or golf course, some pubs and connecting streets. That's all. No, I'm wrong, there's also the cinema and the library. And when our imagination needs exercise we use these to visit London, Paris, Rome under the Caesars, the American West at the turn of the century, anywhere but here and now. Imaginatively Glasgow exists as a music-hall song and a few bad novels. That's all we've given to the world outside. It's all we've given to ourselves."

The same apparent contradiction is true of Scotland or anywhere – that it doesn't become a real place until it is lived in imaginatively. In fact, Scotland has been a realm of imagined living more than many other places: the extensive imagination of Sir Walter Scott used Scotland so well in the 19th century that the view of the country and nation that he offered is still resonant, long after the decline of his huge popularity as an author. In his novels he portrayed Scotland as a country emerging from a past of war, lawlessness and division, particularly between Highlands and Lowlands, into a settled and united modernity. Scott wrote with regret for a vanished past, but also with great irony about heroes such as Edward Waverley ("a sneaking piece of imbecility", he called him), infatuated with all things Highland, but the irony was lost on most readers, who lapped up the adventures Scott served them as eagerly and unquestioningly as if they were Waverleys too. The intelligence of Scott's work was obscured by a mist of romance, and increasingly, and despite many imitators, his view became less and less relevant to the daily lives of the actual inhabitants of industrialised, urban Scotland. Tom Buchan's 'Scotland the wee' is actually a satirical take on Scott's famously patriotic lines from *The Lay of the Last Minstrel*:

> O Caledonia, stern and wild,
> Meet nurse for a poetic child!
> Land of brown heath and shaggy wood,
> Land of the mountain and the flood...

In many respects, it could be argued that Scottish literature since Scott – from the sentimental Celtic Twilight poets and Kailyard novelists of the late 19th century, through the MacDiarmid-led Literary Renaissance of the 1920s and 1930s, to the "proletarian romanticism" (the late Alan Bold's phrase) of novelists like William McIlvanney and the post-industrial dirty realism of Irvine Welsh – has been a series of attempts to counter earlier depictions of Scotland and Scottish society. In recent years, poets such as Robert Crawford have tried to offer a vision that is both imaginatively challenging and yet founded in reality:

> Semiconductor country, land crammed with intimate expanses,
> Your cities are superlattices, heterojunctive
> Graphed from the air, your cropmarked farmlands
> Are epitaxies of tweed.
>
> All night motorways carry your signal, swept
> To East Kilbride or Dunfermline. A brightness off low headlands
> Beams-in the dawn to Fife's interstices,
> Optoelectronics of hay.
>
> *Scotland*

In the 1980s and 1990s, partly in response to the immense sense of political failure and cultural insecurity felt around the 1979 devolution referendum, a wave of writers – far too many even to list here – began to do what those characters in Alasdair Gray's *Lanark* discuss: to use Scotland imaginatively, to reassess and repossess it imaginatively; to suggest that many Scotlands might exist within its geographical bounds. Not only were stereotypical ideas of Scotland challenged, but so were stereotypical ideas of what or who a Scottish writer might be. The most exciting thing about recent Scottish literature is its sheer diversity of voice, accent, language, ethnicity, genre, style, sexuality – and not least the much increased publication of women writers. Here, for example, is Christine de Luca, writing in Shetland dialect of change and continuity, both geological and human, in her poem 'Da Fremd' ('The Outsiders'):

> An still we wander, come an geng
> muv'd bi forces oot a wir control
> fin wirsels lodged in uncan pairts.
> Da ooter layers, dey bruckle
> peerie-wyes: wear doon, roond aff;
> but no da inner places o da hert.

Perhaps what characterises the category "Scottish writing" more than anything these days is a refusal to be easily categorised. Which is why the appointment of Edwin Morgan as Scotland's Makar or poet laureate was so appropriate. For Morgan, over six decades, has been publishing work that has always been varied, restless, optimistic, intelligent, inquisitive and interested, as in this poem of strange discovery from his 1984 collection *Sonnets from Scotland*:

> We brushed the dirt off, held it to the light.
> The obverse showed us *Scotland*, and the head
> of a red deer; the antler-glint had fled
> but the fine cut could still be felt. All right:
> we turned it over, read easily *One Pound*,

but then the shock of Latin, like a gloss,
Respublica Scotorum, sent across
such ages as we guessed but never found
at the worn edge where once the date had been
and where as many fingers had gripped hard
as hopes their silent race had lost or gained.
The marshy scurf crept up to our machine,
sucked at our boots. Yet nothing seemed ill-starred.
And least of all the realm the coin contained.

The Coin

Is it possible that, as with our writers, in a 21st-century, democratic and multi-voiced Scotland the best thing about our national identity is that it cannot be readily pigeon-holed? We need our history, to be aware of it and to understand it, because it is the story of who we have been and where we have come from, but we also need not to be restrained by it:

What do you mean when you speak of Scotland?
The grey defeats that are dead and gone
behind the legends each generation
savours, yet can't live on?

Inheritance of guilt that our country
has never stood where we feel she should?
A nagging threat of unfinished struggle
somehow forever lost in the blood?

Scotland's a sense of change, an endless
becoming for which there was never a kind
of wholeness or ultimate category.
Scotland's an attitude of mind.

Speaking of Scotland

This same idea has been expressed by many writers since Maurice Lindsay published these lines in 1964 – a date which perhaps reminds us that even our supposedly new attitudes of mind are not so new. It seems appropriate to conclude with a passage from one of the most intelligent novels to emerge from the 1980s, *The Other McCoy* by Brian McCabe:

> "Scotland is a state of mind," said McCoy.
>
> "That's very true," said MacRae.
>
> "Who said that?" asked Grogan, suddenly alert.
>
> "You did. At least I think it was you."
>
> "Did I? By Christ, I'll drink to that," said Grogan and he poured the last of the half-bottle into their glasses.
>
> "To Scotland as a concept," said MacRae.
>
> "No. A state of mind," corrected Grogan.
>
> "He's right, it's different," said McCoy.
>
> And they all toasted Scotland as a state of mind.

further reading

Alan Bold, *Modern Scottish Literature* (Longman 1983)

Alexander Broadie, *The Scottish Enlightenment* (Birlinn 2001)

Robert Burns, *Poems* (various editions)

James Buchan, *Capital of the Mind: How Edinburgh Changed the World* (John Murray 2003)

John Buchan, *The Power-House* (1916, various editions)

Robert Crawford, *A Scottish Assembly* (Chatto & Windus 1990)

William Dunbar, *Poems* (various editions)

Robert Fergusson, *Selected Poems* (edited by James Robertson, Birlinn 2000)

Matthew Fitt & James Robertson (editors), *The Smoky Smirr o Rain* (Itchy Coo 2003)

John Galt, *The Provost* (1822, various editions)

Robert Garioch, *Complete Poetical Works* (edited by Robin Fulton, Polygon 2004)

Douglas Gifford & Alan Riach (editors), *Scotlands: Poets and the Nation* (Carcanet 2004)

Alasdair Gray, *Lanark* (Canongate 1981)

James Hogg, *The Private Memoirs and Confessions of a Justified Sinner* (1824, various editions)

R.D.S. Jack & Pat Rozendal, *The Mercat Anthology of Early Scottish Literature 1375–1707* (Mercat Press 1997)

Kathleen Jamie, *Jizzen* (Picador 1999)

Maurice Lindsay (editor), *Scotland: An Anthology* (Robert Hale 1974)

Liz Lochhead, *Mary Queen of Scots Got Her Head Chopped Off* (Penguin 1989)

Christine de Luca, *Wast wi da Valkyries* (Shetland Library 1997)

Sir David Lyndsay, *Ane Satyre of the Thrie Estaitis* (Canongate 1989)

Brian McCabe, *The Other McCoy* (Mainstream 1990)

Norman MacCaig, *The Poems of Norman MacCaig*
(edited by Ewen McCaig, Polygon 2005)

Hugh MacDiarmid, *Selected Prose* (edited by Alan Riach, Carcanet 1992)

Hugh MacDiarmid, *Complete Poems*
(edited by Michael Grieve & Alan Riach, Carcanet 1993–4)

Sorley MacLean, *Dàin do Eimhir/Songs to Eimhir*
(edited by Christopher Whyte, Association for Scottish Literary Studies 2002)

Edwin Morgan, *Collected Poems* (Carcanet 1990)

Edwin Morgan, *Sonnets from Scotland* (Mariscat Press 1984)

Trevor Royle, *The Mainstream Companion to Scottish Literature*
(Mainstream 1993)

Sir Walter Scott, *Waverley* (1814, various editions)

Sir Walter Scott, *Guy Mannering* (1815, various editions)

Sir Walter Scott, *The Antiquary* (1816, various editions)

Sir Walter Scott, *The Heart of Midlothian* (1818, various editions)

Sydney Goodsir Smith, *Collected Poems* (John Calder 1975)

William Soutar, *Selected Poems*
(edited by W.J. Aitken, Scottish Academic Press 1988)

Robert Louis Stevenson, *Stevenson's Scotland*
(edited by Tom Hubbard & Duncan Glen, Mercat Press 2004).
Includes the complete text of *Edinburgh: Picturesque Notes*

Jacqueline Tasioulas (editor), *The Makars: An Anthology* (Canongate 1999)

Roderick Watson, *The Literature of Scotland* (Macmillan 1984)

Roderick Watson (editor), *The Poetry of Scotland*
(Edinburgh University Press 1995)

afterword

Strange to say, a parliament is not just a building. It's also an assembly of people. People who in turn represent other people, and through them, a country, a nation.

So it is with the Scottish Parliament. But while it may have been controversial during construction, there is no doubt now as to the significance of its fact, form and location.

Looking through Enric Miralles's first sketches – many of which are included here – it is clear just how much inspiration he took from the topology of the site. This interest is inscribed in the building in a variety of ways, signalled in the 'subtle game of views and implications' that James Robertson identifies and takes up at the beginning of his sonnet sequence. It runs like a thread through the content and design of this book. Here, poems and building match each other in a dialogue that takes in symbolism and geography, history, form and aspiration. Three short essays deepen this dialogue, situating the theme by providing a context of historical time and place.

There are other inscriptions too, on and in the body of the building, not least the words of Scottish writers visible on the Canongate side. The intention of this short residency or intervention was to ensure that the literature represented by those words, with its distinguished history and distinctive insights, was brought alive to the people inside: the parliamentarians, their research staff, and all those who work there – security, cleaners, caterers and so on. It was in one sense a transmogrification into and a christening of the new building.

Equally, the intention of this publication is to ensure a wider public access for the powerful new work created by James Robertson, and the ideas and themes that inform it. These have a national significance. Literature is at the heart of this nation; it is a bread that can and should be broken, shared and enjoyed by everyone. Quite apart from the fact that it is indisputably ours, and that it carries our languages and our histories, it is also the arena in which we can continually re-examine and reshape ourselves. Just as these poems echo the shapes of the parliament building, so literature echoes the historical and social affairs of the people in it.

That was our ethos. Because literature, like a parliament, has the capacity to give us back to ourselves better, new, re-imagined.

Marc Lambert
Scottish Book Trust

Scottish **Book** Trust

Scottish Book Trust is Scotland's national agency for readers and writers.

We exist to bring books and people together by providing key services to readers, writers and the educational sector.

We provide:

Independent advice and information for readers and writers

Free reading related resources

Support for writers and the development of writing in Scotland

Quality resources to the educational and libraries sector

Readership development and education programmes

National author tours and events

Live Literature Scotland funding for author events in schools and communities

Find out more: **www.scottishbooktrust.com**
or contact us at
**Scottish Book Trust, Sandeman House, Trunk's Close,
55 High Street, Edinburgh EH1 1SR**

Tel **0131 524 0160**
Fax **0131 524 0161**
Email **info@scottishbooktrust.com**

Patron **Alexander McCall Smith**

Registered Charity No. **SCO27669**

Scottish
Arts Council

Luath Press Limited
committed to publishing well written books worth reading

LUATH PRESS takes its name from Robert Burns, whose little collie Luath (*Gael.*, swift or nimble) tripped up Jean Armour at a wedding and gave him the chance to speak to the woman who was to be his wife and the abiding love of his life. Burns called one of *The Twa Dogs* Luath after Cuchullin's hunting dog in *Ossian's Fingal*. Luath Press was established in 1981 in the heart of Burns country, and is now based a few steps up the road from Burns' first lodgings on Edinburgh's Royal Mile. Luath offers you distinctive writing with a hint of unexpected pleasures.

Most bookshops in the UK, the US, Canada, Australia, New Zealand and parts of Europe either carry our books in stock or can order them for you. To order direct from us, please send a £sterling cheque, postal order, international money order or your credit card details (number, address of cardholder and expiry date) to us at the address below. Please add post and packing as follows: UK – £1.00 per delivery address; overseas surface mail – £2.50 per delivery address; overseas airmail – £3.50 for the first book to each delivery address, plus £1.00 for each additional book by airmail to the same address. If your order is a gift, we will happily enclose your card or message at no extra charge.

Luath Press Limited
543/2 Castlehill
The Royal Mile
Edinburgh EH1 2ND
Scotland
Telephone: 0131 225 4326 (24 hours)
Fax: 0131 225 4324
email: gavin.macdougall@luath.co.uk
Website: www.luath.co.uk